CONTENTS

- 2 INTRODUCTION TO FINGERSTYLE GUITAR
- 3 ALL THE THINGS YOU ARE
- 6 ALL THE WAY
- 9 BUT BEAUTIFUL
- 12 COME RAIN OR COME SHINE
- 15 FOR ALL WE KNOW
- 18 I DON'T KNOW WHY (I JUST DO)
- 20 I'LL BE AROUND
- 23 I'LL KNOW
- 26 LOVE LETTERS
- 30 MY ONE AND ONLY LOVE
- 33 THE NEARNESS OF YOU
- 36 PEOPLE WILL SAY WE'RE IN LOVE
- 39 THEY SAY IT'S WONDERFUL
- 42 TIME AFTER TIME
- 45 TO LOVE AND BE LOVED

ISBN 978-1-4234-1648-7

7777 W. BLUEMOUND RD. P.O. BOX 13819 MILWAUKEE, WI 53213

For all works contained herein:
Unauthorized copying, arranging, adapting, recording, Internet posting,
public performance, or other distribution of the printed music in this publication is an infringement of copyright.
Infringers are liable under the law.

Visit Hal Leonard Online at
www.halleonard.com

INTRODUCTION TO FINGERSTYLE GUITAR

Fingerstyle (a.k.a. fingerpicking) is a guitar technique that means you literally pick the strings with your right-hand fingers and thumb. This contrasts with the conventional technique of strumming and playing single notes with a pick (a.k.a. flatpicking). For fingerpicking, you can use any type of guitar: acoustic steel-string, nylon-string classical, or electric.

THE RIGHT HAND

The most common right-hand position is shown here.

Use a high wrist; arch your palm as if you were holding a ping-pong ball. Keep the thumb outside and away from the fingers, and let the fingers do the work rather than lifting your whole hand.

The thumb generally plucks the bottom strings with downstrokes on the left side of the thumb and thumbnail. The other fingers pluck the higher strings using upstrokes with the fleshy tip of the fingers and fingernails. The thumb and fingers should pluck one string per stroke and not brush over several strings.

Another picking option you may choose to use is called hybrid picking (a.k.a. plectrum-style fingerpicking). Here, the pick is usually held between the thumb and first finger, and the three remaining fingers are assigned to pluck the higher strings.

THE LEFT HAND

The left-hand fingers are numbered 1 through 4.

Be sure to keep your fingers arched, with each joint bent; if they flatten out across the strings, they will deaden the sound when you fingerpick. As a general rule, let the strings ring as long as possible when playing fingerstyle.

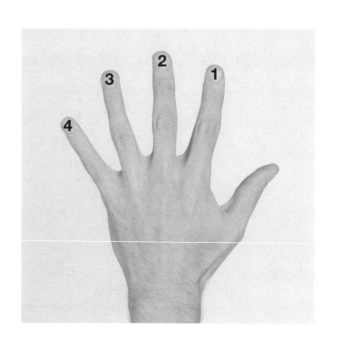

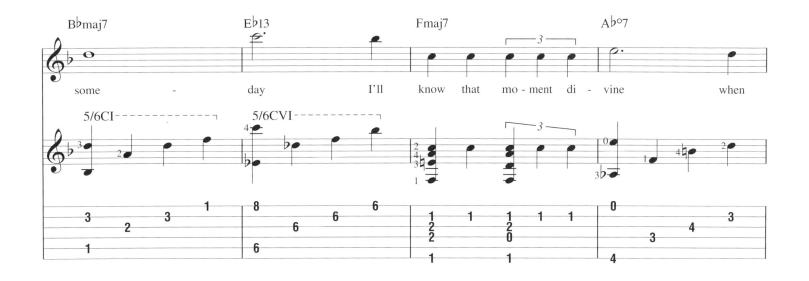
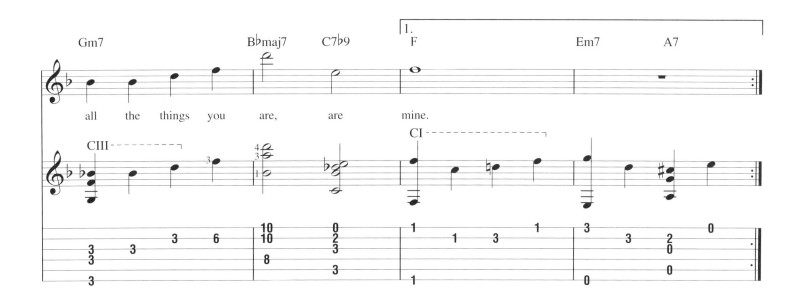
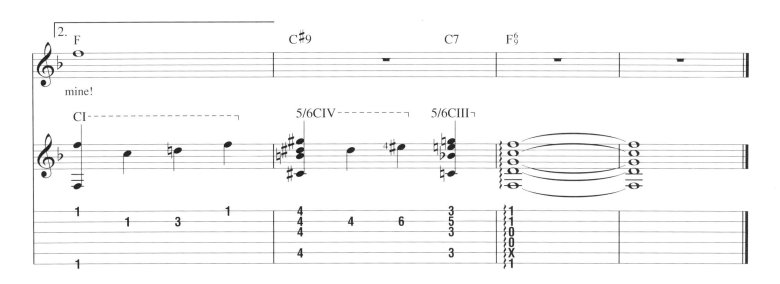

5

All the Way
from THE JOKER IS WILD
Words by Sammy Cahn
Music by James Van Heusen

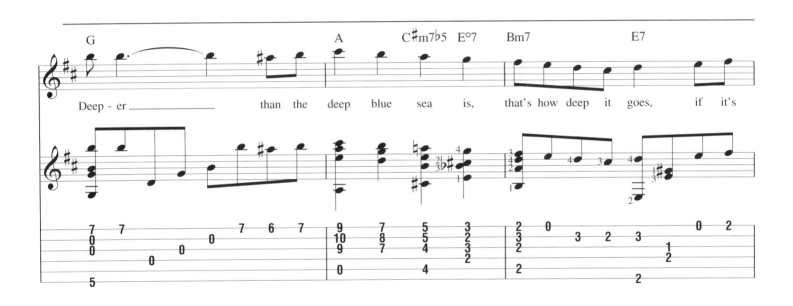
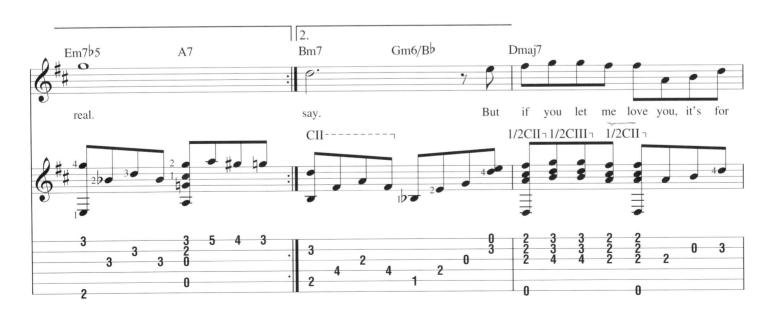

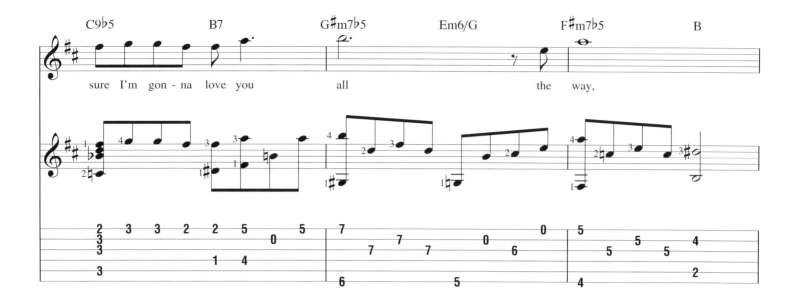

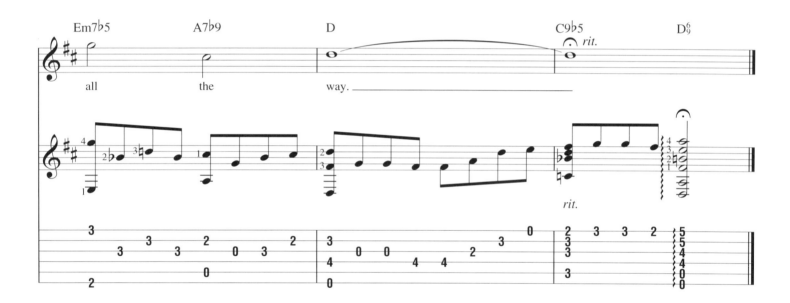

Additional Lyrics

2. When somebody needs you,
   It's no good unless he needs you all the way.
   Through the good or lean years
   And for all those in between years, come what may.
   Who knows where the road will lead us,
   Only a fool would say.
   But if you let me love you,
   It's for sure I'm gonna love you all the way,
   All the way.

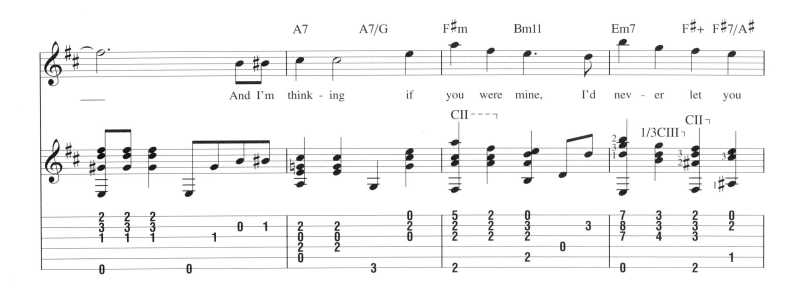
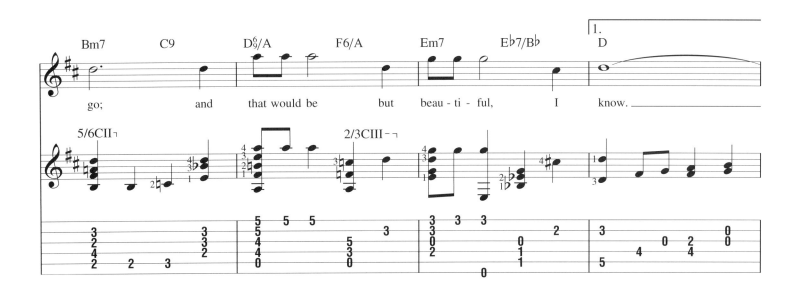
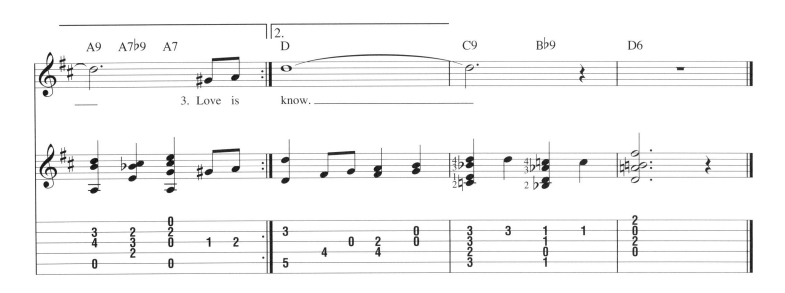

Come Rain or Come Shine

from ST. LOUIS WOMAN
Words by Johnny Mercer
Music by Harold Arlen

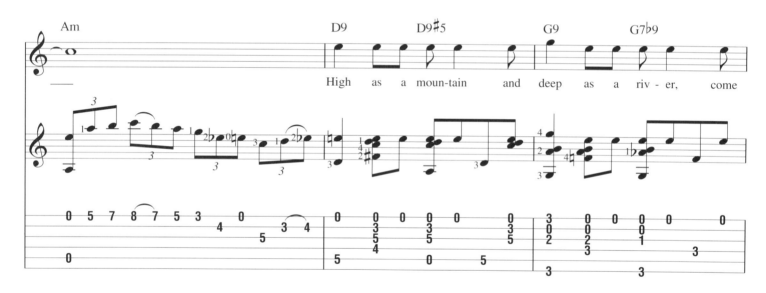

Copyright © 1946 (Renewed) by Chappell & Co. and S.A. Music Co.
This arrangement Copyright © 2012 by Chappell & Co. and S.A. Music Co.
International Copyright Secured   All Rights Reserved

For All We Know

Words by Sam M. Lewis
Music by J. Fred Coots

Copyright © 1934 (Renewed) and 1956 (Renewed) by Sis 'N Bro Music Company and Toy Town Tunes, Inc., Boca Raton, FL
This arrangement Copyright © 2012 by Sis 'N Bro Music Company and Toy Town Tunes, Inc.
International Copyright Secured   All Rights Reserved
Used by Permission

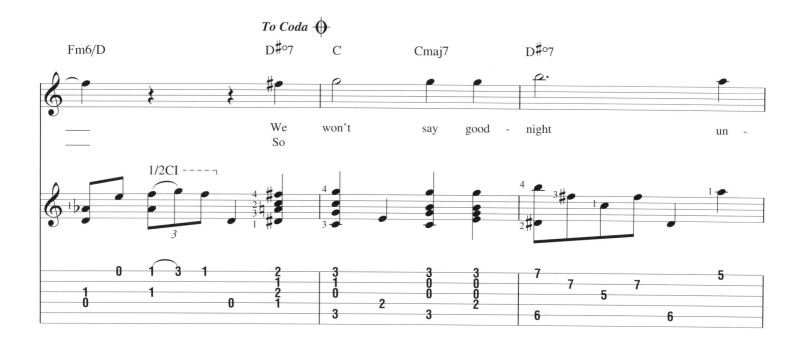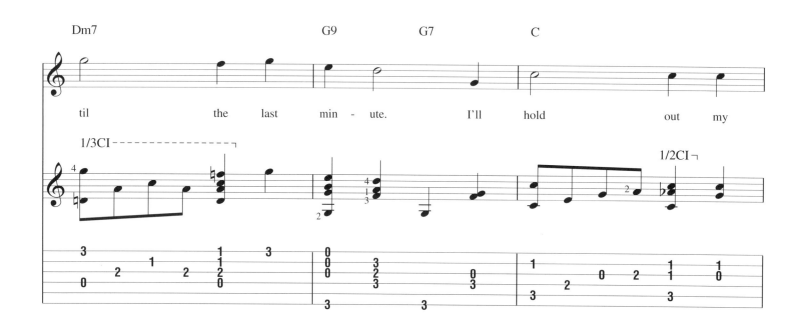

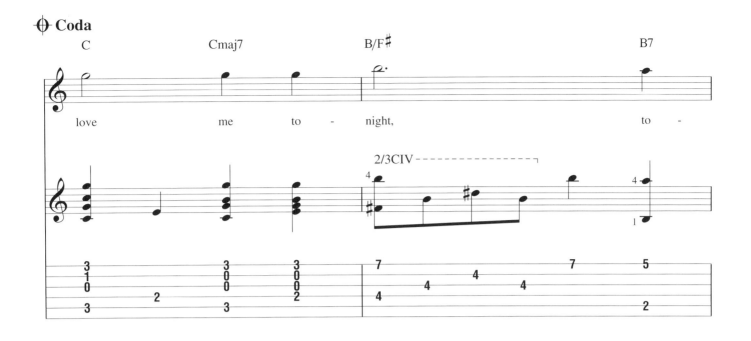
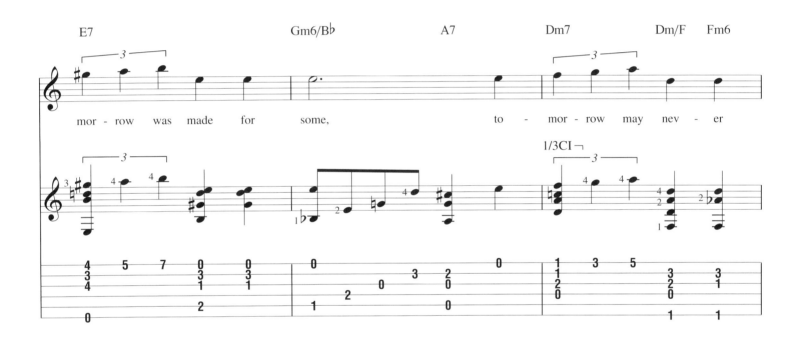
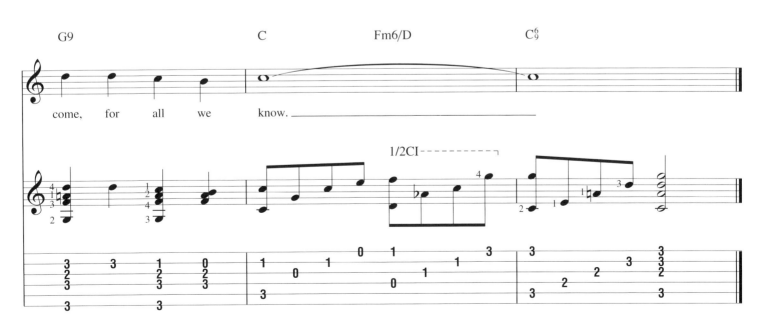

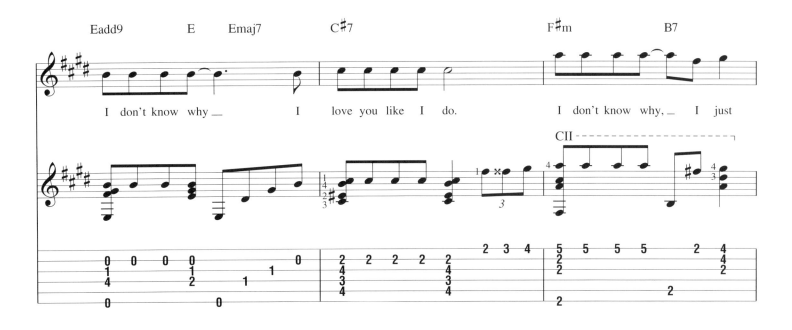

19

I'll Be Around

Words and Music by Alec Wilder

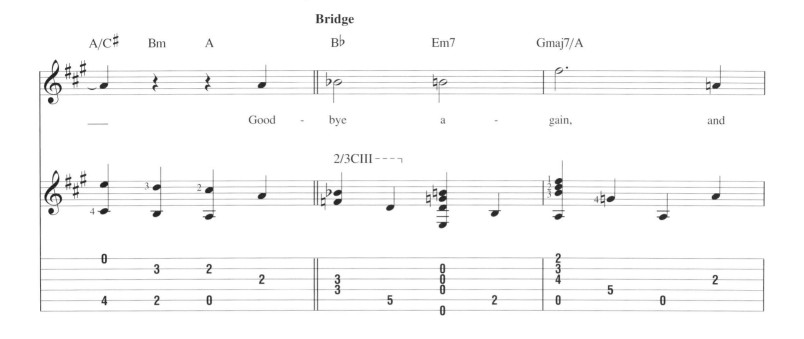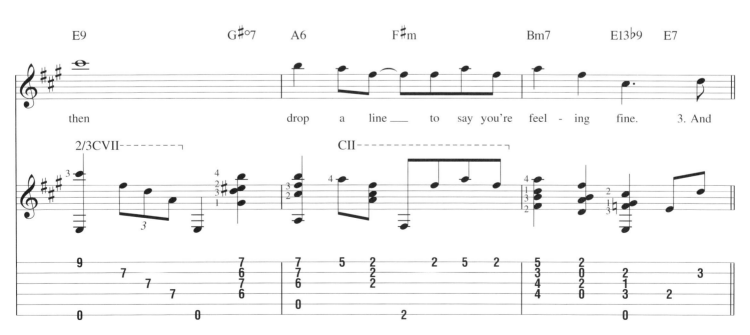

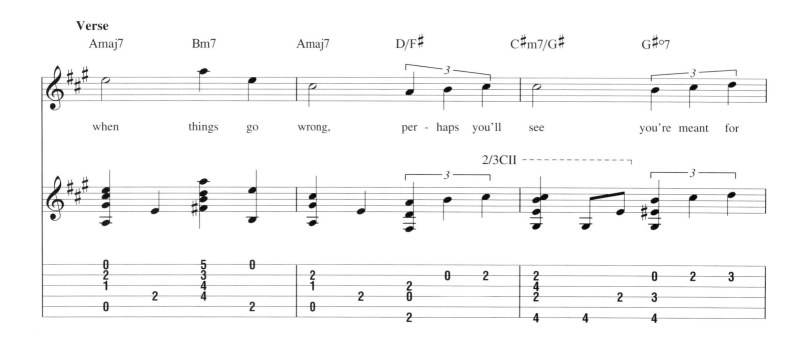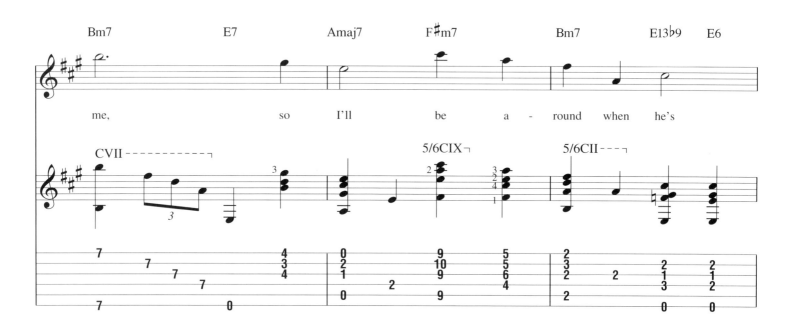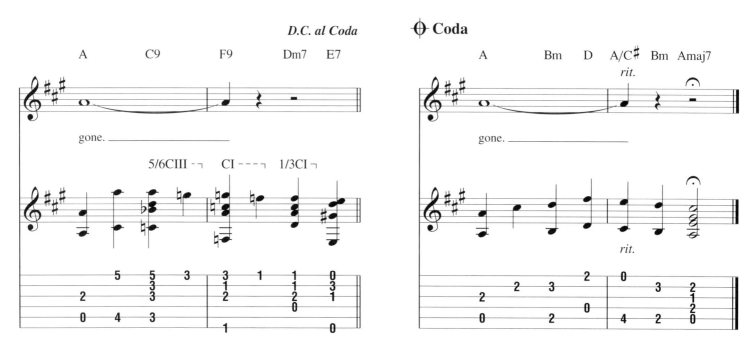

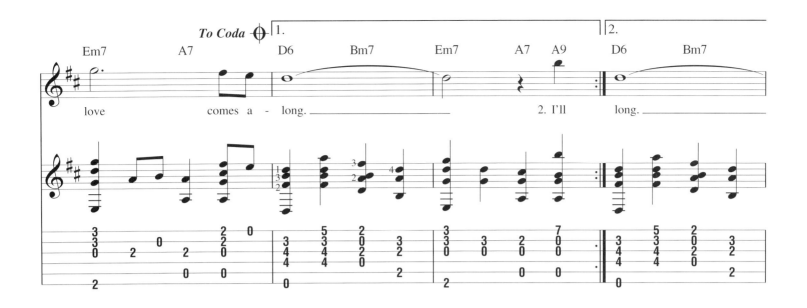
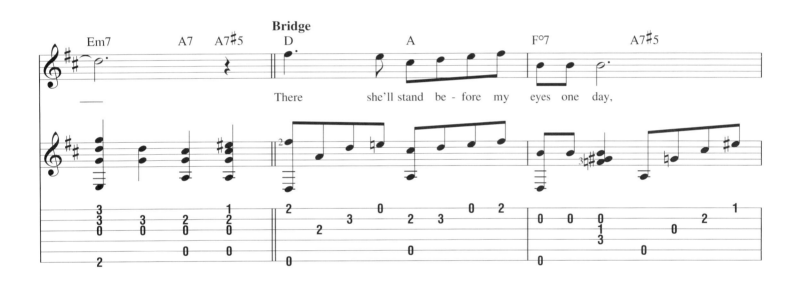

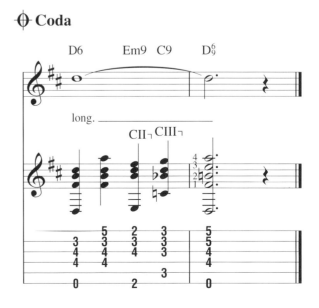

Love Letters
Theme from the Paramount Picture LOVE LETTERS
Words by Edward Heyman
Music by Victor Young

Drop D tuning:
(low to high) D-A-D-G-B-E

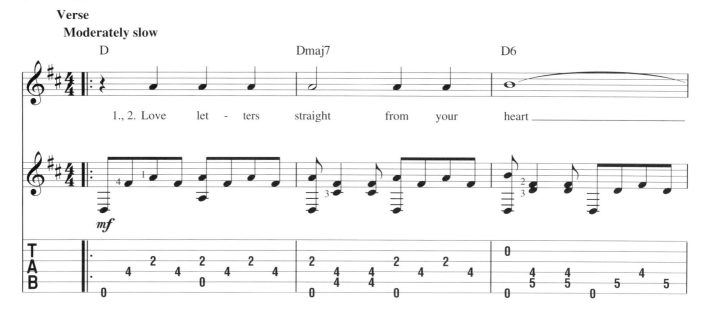

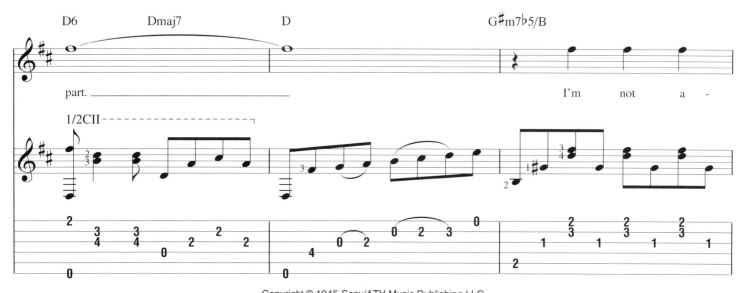

Copyright © 1945 Sony/ATV Music Publishing LLC
Copyright Renewed
This arrangement Copyright © 2012 Sony/ATV Music Publishing LLC
All Rights Administered by Sony/ATV Music Publishing LLC, 8 Music Square West, Nashville, TN 37203
International Copyright Secured   All Rights Reserved

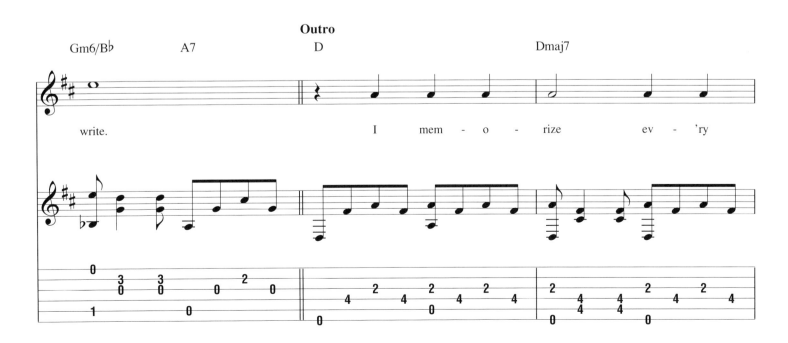

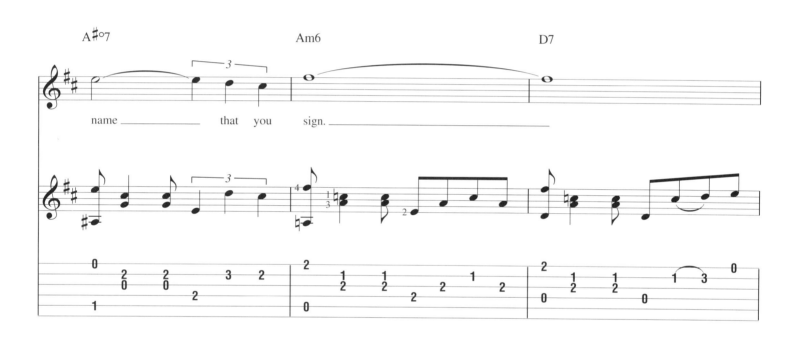

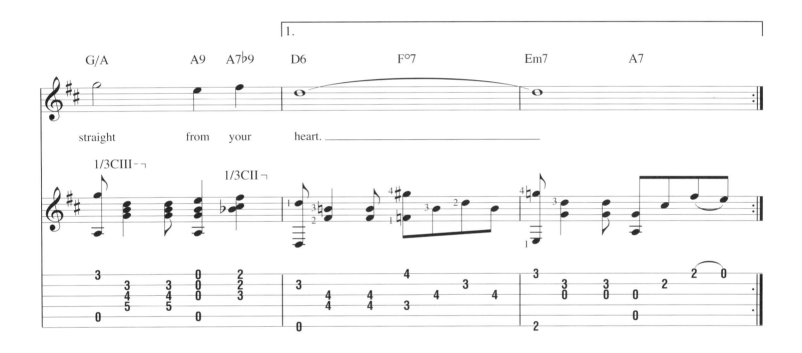
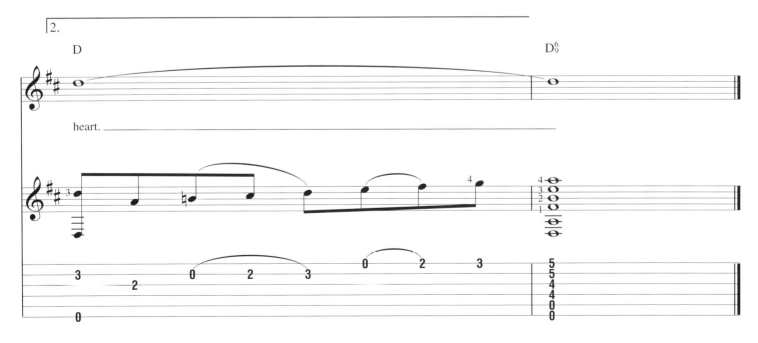

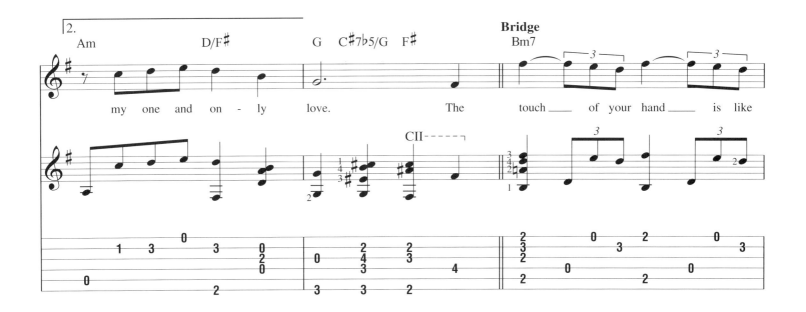

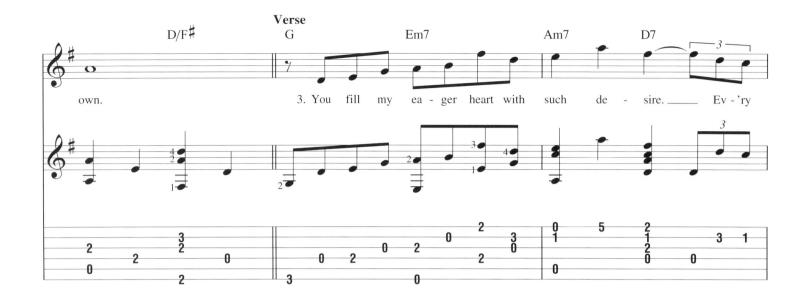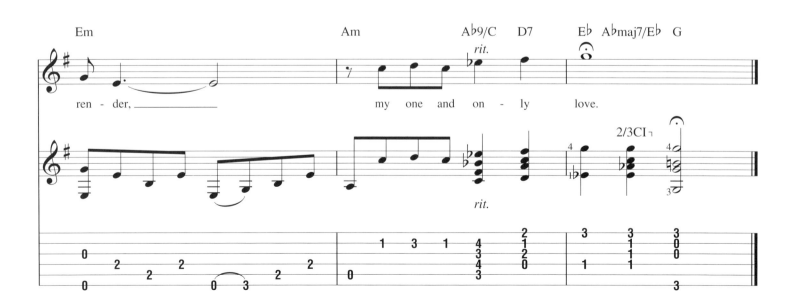

The Nearness of You
from the Paramount Picture ROMANCE IN THE DARK

Words by Ned Washington
Music by Hoagy Carmichael

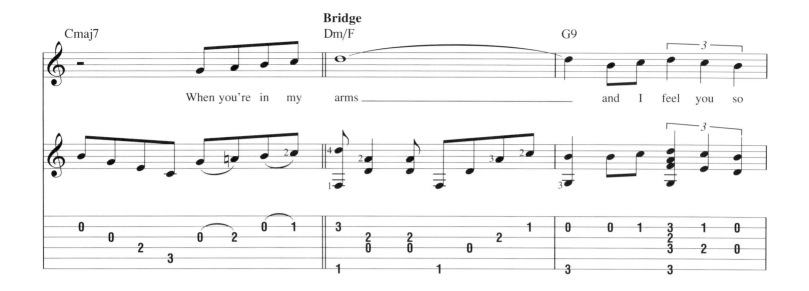
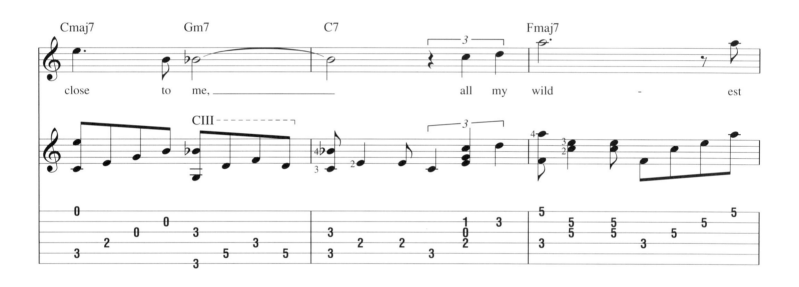
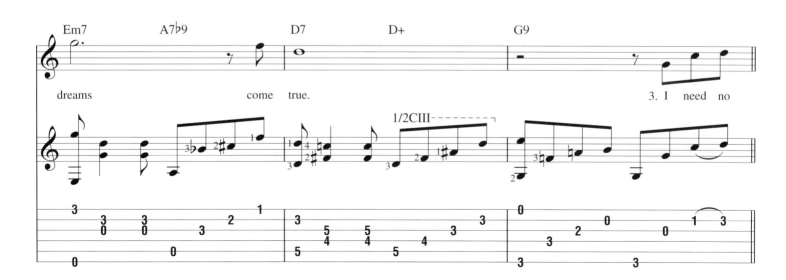

People Will Say We're in Love

from OKLAHOMA!
Lyrics by Oscar Hammerstein II
Music by Richard Rodgers

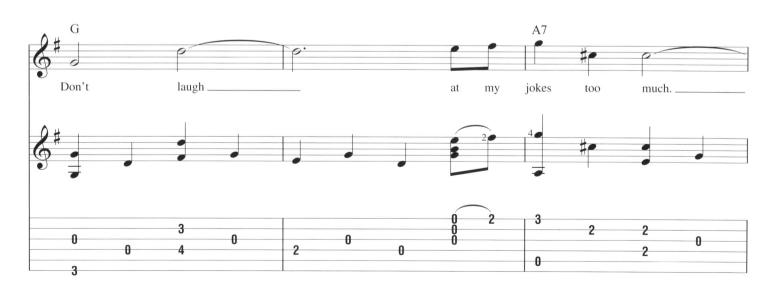

Copyright © 1943 by Williamson Music, a Division of Rodgers & Hammerstein: an Imagem Company
Copyright Renewed
This arrangement Copyright © 2012 by Williamson Music, a Division of Rodgers & Hammerstein: an Imagem Company
International Copyright Secured All Rights Reserved

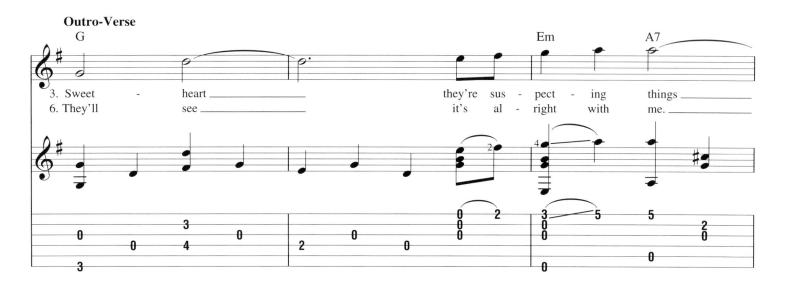
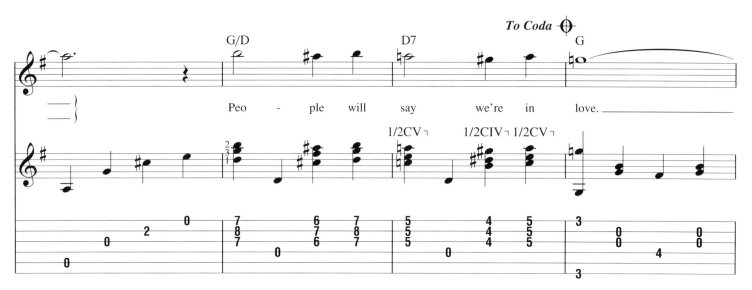
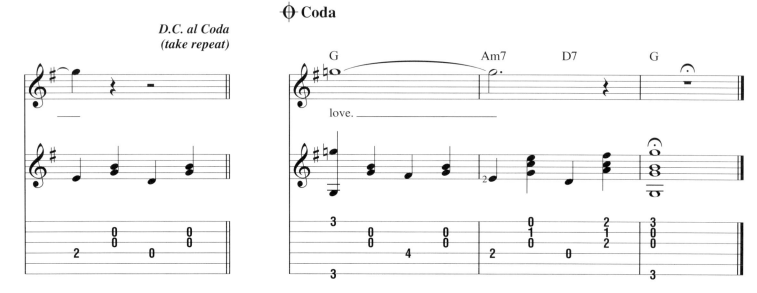

Additional Lyrics

2. Don't sigh and gaze at me.
   Your sighs are so like mine.
   Your eyes mustn't glow like mine.
   People will say we're in love!

4. Don't praise my charm too much.
   Don't look so vain with me.
   Don't stand in the rain with me.
   People will say we're in love!

5. Don't take my arm too much.
   Don't keep your hand in mine.
   Your hand feels so grand in mine.
   People will say we're in love!

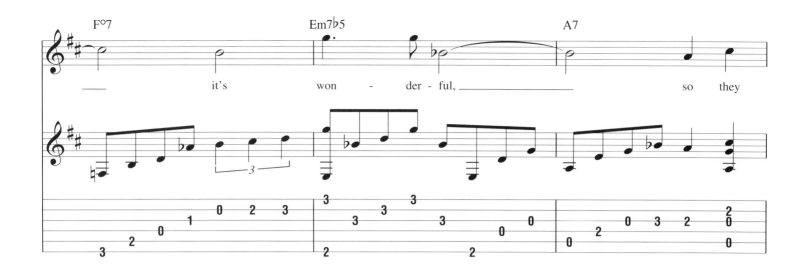
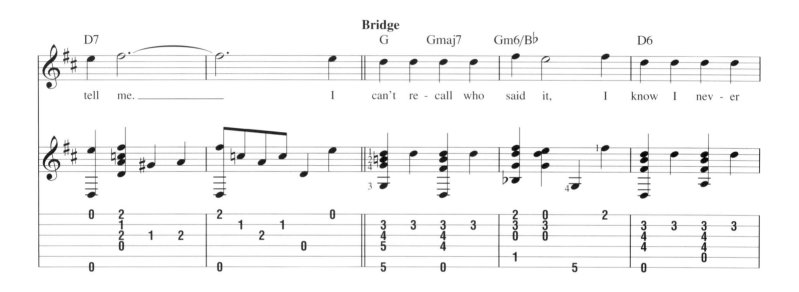

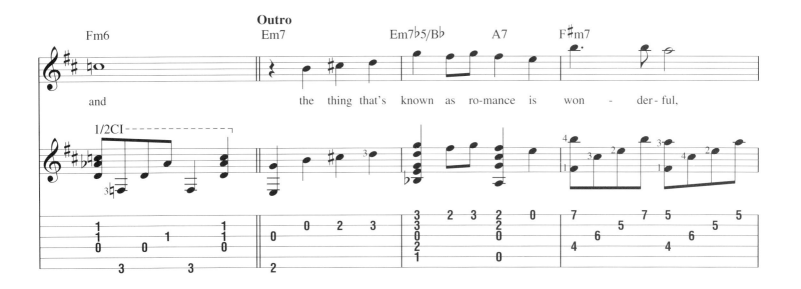
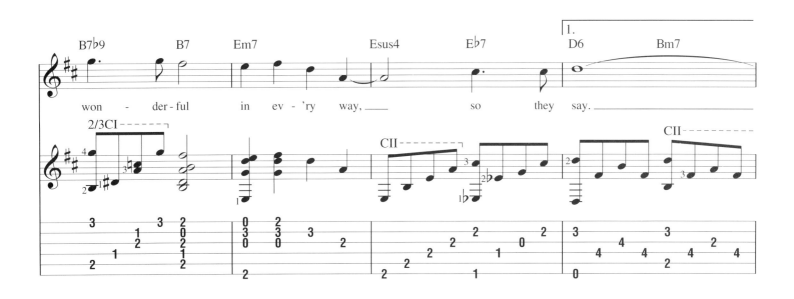
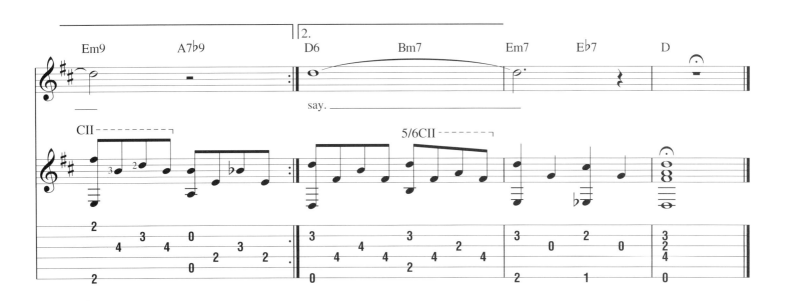

Time After Time
from the Metro-Goldwyn-Mayer Picture IT HAPPENED IN BROOKLYN
Words by Sammy Cahn
Music by Jule Styne

42

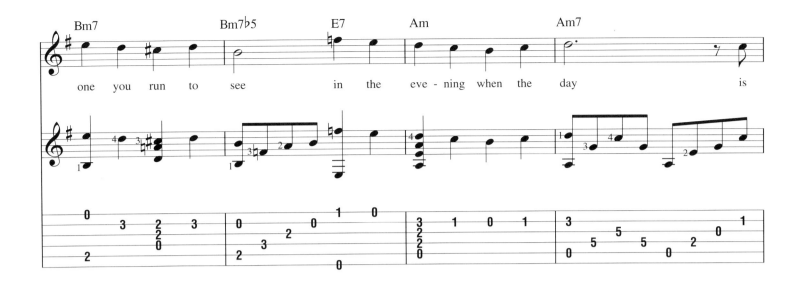
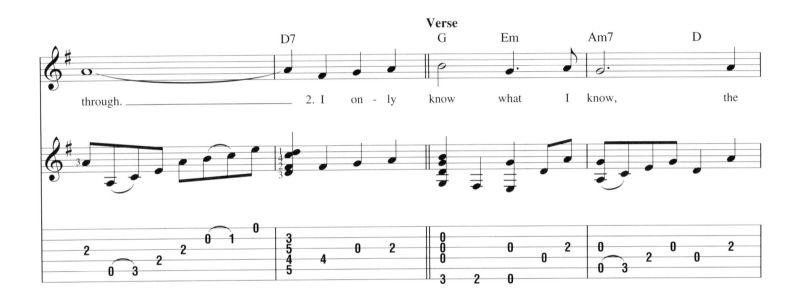

43

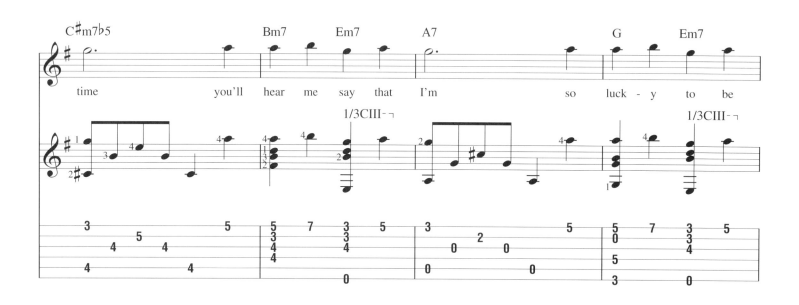
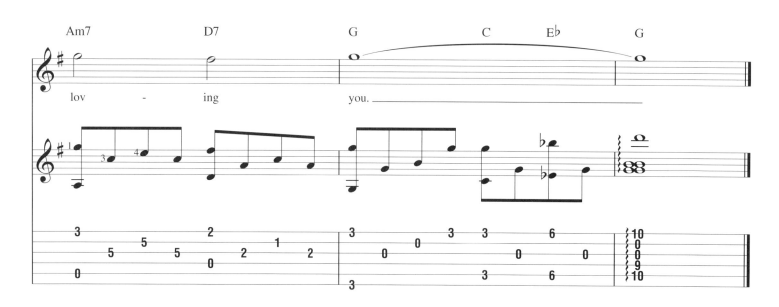

To Love and Be Loved
from the film SOME CAME RUNNING

Words by Sammy Cahn
Music by James Van Heusen

Copyright © 1958 (Renewed) Maraville Music Corp.
This arrangement Copyright © 2012 Maraville Music Corp.
All Rights Reserved   Used by Permission

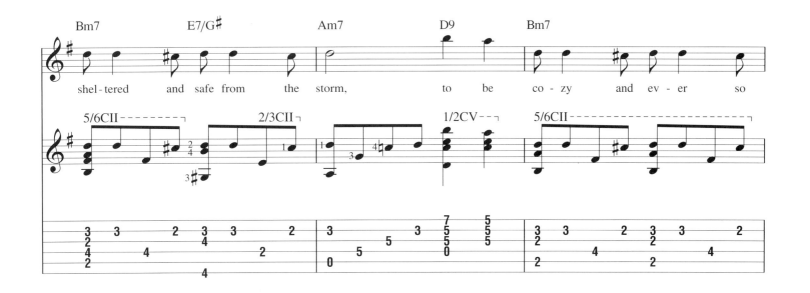
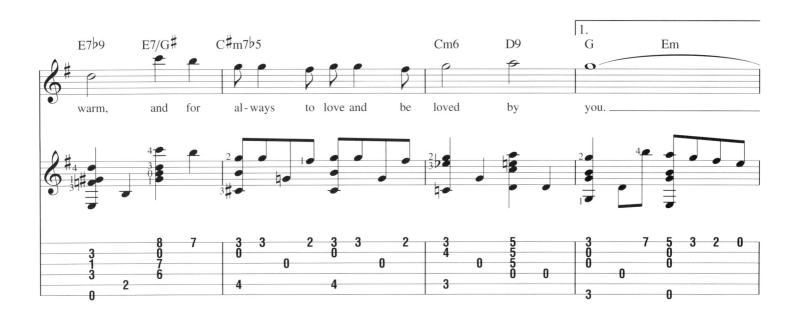
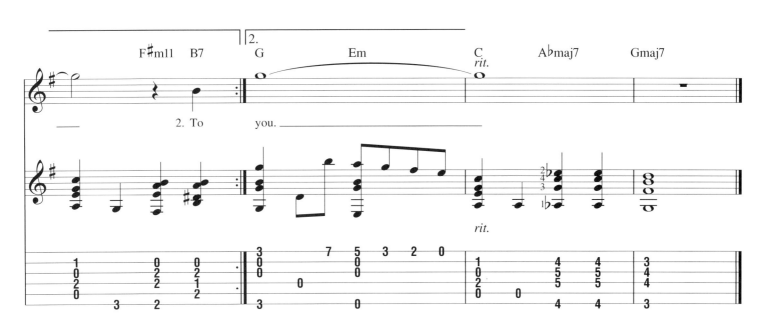

47

FINGERPICKING GUITAR BOOKS

Hone your fingerpicking skills with these great songbooks featuring solo guitar arrangements in standard notation and tablature. The arrangements in these books are carefully written for intermediate-level guitarists. Each song combines melody and harmony in one superb guitar fingerpicking arrangement. Each book also includes an introduction to basic fingerstyle guitar.

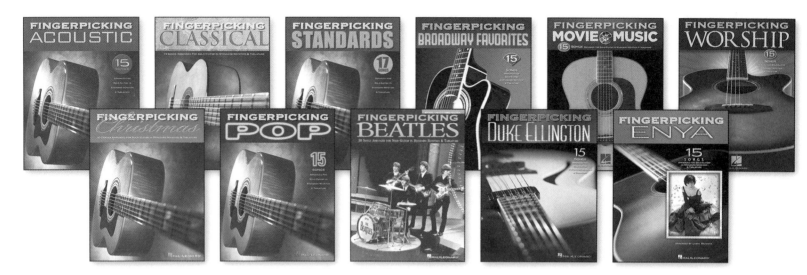

FINGERPICKING ACOUSTIC
00699614...$10.99

FINGERPICKING ACOUSTIC ROCK
00699764...$9.99

FINGERPICKING BACH
00699793...$8.95

FINGERPICKING BALLADS
00699717...$9.99

FINGERPICKING BEATLES
00699049...$19.99

FINGERPICKING BROADWAY FAVORITES
00699843...$9.99

FINGERPICKING BROADWAY HITS
00699838...$7.99

FINGERPICKING CELTIC FOLK
00701148...$7.99

FINGERPICKING CHILDREN'S SONGS
00699712...$9.99

FINGERPICKING CHRISTMAS
00699599...$8.95

FINGERPICKING CHRISTMAS CLASSICS
00701695...$7.99

FINGERPICKING CLASSICAL
00699620...$8.95

FINGERPICKING COUNTRY
00699687...$9.99

FINGERPICKING DISNEY
00699711...$10.99

FINGERPICKING DUKE ELLINGTON
00699845...$9.99

FINGERPICKING ENYA
00701161...$9.99

FINGERPICKING GOSPEL
00701059...$7.99

FINGERPICKING HYMNS
00699688...$8.95

FINGERPICKING IRISH SONGS
00701965...$7.99

FINGERPICKING JAZZ STANDARDS
00699840...$7.99

FINGERPICKING LATIN STANDARDS
00699837...$7.99

FINGERPICKING ANDREW LLOYD WEBBER
00699839...$9.99

FINGERPICKING LOVE SONGS
00699841...$7.99

FINGERPICKING LULLABYES
00701276...$9.99

FINGERPICKING MOVIE MUSIC
00699919...$9.99

FINGERPICKING MOZART
00699794...$8.95

FINGERPICKING POP
00699615...$9.99

FINGERPICKING PRAISE
00699714...$8.95

FINGERPICKING ROCK
00699716...$9.99

FINGERPICKING STANDARDS
00699613...$9.99

FINGERPICKING WEDDING
00699637...$9.99

FINGERPICKING WORSHIP
00700554...$7.99

FINGERPICKING NEIL YOUNG – GREATEST HITS
00700134...$12.99

FINGERPICKING YULETIDE
00699654...$9.99

HAL•LEONARD® CORPORATION
7777 W. BLUEMOUND RD. P.O. BOX 13819 MILWAUKEE, WI 53213

Visit Hal Leonard online at www.halleonard.com

Prices, contents and availability subject to change without notice.